Grover Cleveland

Grover Cleveland

Betsy Ochester

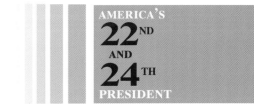

AMERICA'S
22ND
AND
24TH
PRESIDENT

Children's Press®
A Division of Scholastic Inc.
New York / Toronto / London / Auckland / Sydney
Mexico City / New Delhi / Hong Kong
Danbury, Connecticut

Library of Congress Cataloging-in-Publication Data

Ochester, Betsy.
    Grover Cleveland / by Betsy Ochester.
        p. cm. — (Encyclopedia of presidents. Second series)
Includes bibliographical references and index.
    ISBN 0-516-22962-1
    1. Cleveland, Grover, 1837–1908—Juvenile literature. 2. Presidents—United
States—Biography—Juvenile literature. [1. Cleveland, Grover, 1837–1908.
2. Presidents.] I. Title. II. Series.
E697.O28 2004
973.8'5'092—dc22   2003027246

Contents

Chapter 1

Don't Rock the Boat ——————

It was a day cloaked in secrecy. During the afternoon, a group of the country's best physicians boarded a steam yacht named *Oneida*, which was docked in New York City's East River, and disappeared below deck. Later, a large, burly man climbed aboard. He sat down in a chair on deck and began a good-natured chat with a friend. His name was Grover Cleveland, and he was president of the United States.

At that moment in the summer of 1893, the president had the weight of the world on his broad shoulders. The United States was gripped in a financial panic. Hundreds of banks had closed, and some 2 million people were unemployed. Funds in the nation's treasury had dipped dangerously low. The country was relying on President Cleveland to help business restore confidence and get the nation moving again.

In 1893, surgeons on board the steam yacht *Oneida* removed a cancerous growth from President Cleveland's mouth as the yacht sailed slowly through Long Island Sound. The operation was kept secret for more than 25 years.

Why was he in New York on this warm afternoon? The truth was that President Cleveland was facing another crisis that required immediate attention. Weeks earlier, doctors had confirmed that a growth on the roof of his mouth was cancerous. If it was not removed quickly, his life would be in danger. Below deck, surgeons were preparing to perform surgery the next morning as the yacht steamed slowly up the East River and into Long Island Sound.

The president and his advisers insisted that the operation be performed in secret. If the country found out that the president had cancer, the financial panic could get worse. The nation could face ruin. Would Cleveland survive the operation? Would he recover and have the strength to guide the nation through troubled times? He had already accomplished amazing things. For one, he was the first president to win the presidency, lose it, and win it again. Now, only time would tell if he could recover and complete his second term.

Beginnings

The yacht *Oneida* was docked that day only 20 miles (32 kilometers) from President Cleveland's birthplace in Caldwell, New Jersey. He was born there on March 18, 1837. The fifth of nine children born to the Reverend Richard Cleveland and his wife, Ann, he was christened Stephen Grover Cleveland. As a boy and young man, the future president was known as Steve. Later, he dropped his first name and was known as Grover Cleveland.

The house Stephen was born in was the manse, a house at 207 Bloomfield Avenue owned by Caldwell's Presbyterian church for the use of its pastor. It was a small house then, and must have been crowded, with five small children and their parents. Years later, it was enlarged, and today it houses a museum honoring its most famous resident, President Grover Cleveland.

Grover Cleveland was born in this house in Caldwell, New Jersey, in 1837. The house was much smaller when the Cleveland family lived there and was enlarged only after they moved away.

The Cleveland family didn't live there very long. Four years after Stephen Grover's birth, Reverend Cleveland accepted a call to become the pastor of a church in Fayetteville, New York. Fayetteville was a village in the rolling countryside of western New York, about 8 miles (13 km) from Syracuse. Grover spent most of his childhood in the town and had many fond memories of it. He loved exploring the thick woods and swimming in Limestone Creek. His favorite hobby by far was fishing. It would remain a lifelong passion.

Supporting nine children on the small salary of a pastor presented a challenge. The Clevelands grew their own vegetables, and they relied on their children to help out with chores. As a young boy, Grover helped chop wood (fuel for heating and cooking), carry water from a nearby well or stream, and hoe the garden. He also helped to take care of his younger brothers and sisters.

Discipline in the house was strict. Grover later recalled, "Often as a boy, I was compelled to get out of my warm bed at night, to hang up a hat or other garment which I had left on the floor." Each night, the family read the Bible and prayed. On Sundays they attended morning and evening services. Pastor Cleveland was firm, but he also believed that when chores and study were finished for the day, there should be time for play. The family enjoyed candy pulls and popcorn parties in the kitchen, and games played in the parlor or out on the lawn.

Pastor Cleveland believed strongly in the importance of education for his children—both boys and girls. He had been a brilliant student himself, graduating with high honors from Yale University in 1824, and then studying at the Princeton Theological Seminary. He shared many books with his children, including ones on religion, Latin, and math.

Grover started formal schooling at a small, red frame district schoolhouse and later attended the Fayetteville Academy. His schoolmates remembered him as "chuck full of fun" and as a prankster. "Big Steve" as his friends called him—for he was always large for his age—used to play pranks such as removing villagers' front gates. One night he attached a long rope to the academy's bell and rang it in the middle of the night.

The Clevelands lived just a mile (1.6 km) from the Erie Canal, which connected Lake Erie in the west with the Hudson River in the east. Boats and barges loaded with the area's chief export, rock lime, were a common sight. As a boy, Grover earned extra money for the family by flagging down empty barges for the rock-lime shippers. He got ten cents for each boat he connected with a shipper. When Grover knew a shipment of lime would be ready in the morning, he would get up before dawn to be the first to attract the boats.

When Grover was 13, his father took a higher-paying job as district secretary for the American Home Missionary Society in Clinton, New York, about 40

The Erie Canal crossed New York State from the Hudson River at Albany to Lake Erie near Buffalo. It provided work for many, including the young Grover Cleveland.

miles (64 km) east of Fayetteville. Grover started classes at the Clinton Liberal Institute, a small school with just two teachers. Clinton was also the home of Hamilton College, where Grover's oldest brother William was already enrolled. Grover hoped to follow William to Hamilton. His sister Margaret remembered him at this time as "a lad of rather unusual good sense, who did not yield to impulses—he considered well, and was resourceful—but as a student Grover did not shine."

Within a year, Pastor Cleveland's health began to fail, and he could not continue to work. Suddenly the family faced difficult times. Grover was 14, and it was determined that he would leave school and find a job. In the spring of 1852, he went back to Fayetteville, where a friend of the family, John McVicar, offered him the job of clerk in his general store. Grover would receive room and board and $50 for the first year. He worked long days beginning at five in the morning. After washing his face in a basin or in the horse trough in the village square, Grover opened the store, swept it out, built a fire, and had everything ready for McVicar's arrival at seven o'clock. During the day, he waited on customers and ran errands.

After a year, Grover returned to Clinton hoping to attend Hamilton College. His father's health did not improve, however. In the fall of 1853, the family moved to the nearby village of Holland Patent, where Pastor Cleveland became minister to a small congregation. In September, he preached his first sermon there. Two weeks later, he became critically ill and died.

"My Start in Life"

Grover's dream of going to college was dashed. Now he and his two older brothers had to provide for their mother and younger brothers and sisters. Grover's brother William had gone to teach at the New York Institute for the Blind in New York City. On William's recommendation, Grover was hired as an assistant teacher. The school was a bleak, cold building that took up a large city block. It was more like a prison than a school, run with an iron hand by a cruel superintendent. Grover taught the younger children. In the evening, he and William supervised the boys' dormitory. Grover was disheartened by the inhumane conditions at the school and frustrated that he couldn't change them. After a year, he resigned his post and returned to his mother's house in Holland Patent.

One of the town's wealthy citizens, Ingham Townsend, was impressed by young Grover and believed he should follow in his father's footsteps. Townsend offered to pay for Grover's college education if he promised to become a minister. Grover wanted to go to college, but he didn't want to become a minister, and he didn't want to take the money and then break a promise. Instead, he asked Townsend for a loan of $25 to head west with a friend and look for a job.

Townsend gave him the money and said there was no need to repay it. But twelve years later, Grover repaid the loan with interest, saying, "The loan you made me was my start in life."

Grover and his friend set out to seek their fortune. They boarded a train heading for Cleveland, Ohio. Cleveland may have been a promising city, but Grover had picked it largely because it was named for a distant relative. He had

The Cleveland Tradition

The first direct ancestor of Grover Cleveland arrived in the New World in 1635, only 15 years after the Pilgrims landed. Moses Cleaveland (as the name was then spelled) was an eleven-year-old apprentice from Ipswich in England. Moses' grandson Aaron was a graduate of Harvard and a minister who became a friend of Benjamin Franklin. Aaron's son, also named Aaron, served in the Connecticut legislature in the late 1700s, and introduced a bill there to abolish slavery. He was Grover Cleveland's great-grandfather.

Cleveland, Ohio, was named for Moses Cleaveland, a cousin of the second Aaron. This Moses fought under George Washington in the American Revolution and later served in the Connecticut convention that *ratified* (formally approved) the U.S. Constitution. In 1796, he led an exploring party to the Ohio region for a land company. He helped plan a new settlement on Lake Erie, which took the name "Cleaveland" in his honor. By the 1850s, when Grover set out to visit, Cleveland was the largest city in northern Ohio.

☆ ★ ☆

heard stories about a cousin of his great-grandfather, Moses Cleaveland, after whom the city was named.

The train to Cleveland stopped in Buffalo, New York. Grover and his friend got off so that Grover could pay a quick visit to his uncle Lewis Allen. Grover told his uncle about his plan to pursue law studies in Cleveland. Allen advised his young nephew that it was very risky to go to a strange city with little money. He suggested instead that Grover stay in Buffalo. Allen was a prosperous cattle breeder and merchant, and he was preparing a large chart (or book) documenting the bloodlines of the prize cattle he was breeding. Grover could help with the project. Then Allen would help Grover find a law firm where he could be an assistant and study law. (At the time, most aspiring lawyers learned the law by working in a law firm.) Grover thought the offer over and accepted. Grover's friend continued his own journey to Cleveland with no hard feelings.

Grover's decision proved to be a good one. Buffalo became the town in which he would prove his talents and launch his career, one that would take him further than "Big Steve" could ever have dreamed.

Chapter 2

Study Time

In late December 1855, with cold winds howling up and down the Buffalo streets, Grover Cleveland sat at a desk in the law firm of Rogers, Bowen, and Rogers. It was the first day of his chosen profession, his first day to study law. Henry W. Rogers, the senior member of the firm, approached Cleveland's desk with a large, imposing book, and dropped it with a thud. Pointing to the book, he said, "That's where they all begin." Then he turned and strode away, leaving Cleveland alone at his desk in a corner of the office.

Cleveland peered at the cover to discover Blackstone's *Commentaries on the Law*, the bible of the trade. Without hesitating, he plunged into the weighty book. Hours later, he looked up to realize he was locked in the room alone. The partners and clerks had forgotten him and gone to lunch, locking the door behind them.

"Someday," the young student vowed, "I will be better remembered."

Good to his word, Lewis Allen had recommended Cleveland to Rogers, Bowen, and Rogers, one of the best law firms in the city. Cleveland lived with his uncle's family in the settlement of Black Rock, 2 miles (3 km) from his office. The pleasant square house of stucco and stone overlooked the Niagara River and was surrounded by his uncle's vast farmland.

Gradually, Cleveland began to understand the law. He studied Blackstone with dogged tenacity, browsed other law books, and learned from his work as a clerk for the firm's partners. Within six months, he had saved enough money to move from Black Rock into the city, where he rented a room at a boardinghouse. He would miss the countryside, but he could spend more time working and studying. He wrote to his sister Mary, "My employers assure me, that if I keep on I'll make a lawyer."

In the fall of 1856, Cleveland first volunteered to help in a political campaign. Democrat James Buchanan was running for president, and at age 19, Grover urged the citizens of Buffalo to vote for him. Buchanan was elected. Cleveland would have been shocked to know that the next Democrat to be elected president would win election 28 years later, and his name would be Grover Cleveland!

"Most Promising"

In May 1859, at the age of 22, Cleveland was licensed to practice law in New York State. He decided to stay on at Rogers, Bowen, and Rogers, where he was promoted to senior clerk and paid $1,000 a year, a handsome salary for a young unmarried man. Every month, he mailed some of his pay home to his mother in Holland Patent.

In November 1860, Republican Abraham Lincoln was elected president. Lincoln and the Republicans opposed the spread of slavery to new territories. Southerners feared that Lincoln might force them to give up slavery. They began to secede from the Union (withdraw from the U.S. government) and made plans to form a new Confederate States of America. In April 1861, war broke out between the North (the Union) and the South (the Confederacy). President Lincoln called for volunteers for the Union army, and thousands of young men responded. Grover's oldest brother, William, was newly married and earning little as a Presbyterian minister on Long Island. Two other brothers, Fred and Cecil, signed up and marched off to war. This left Grover as the main supporter of his mother and two youngest sisters, Susan and Rose. He may have felt pressure to join the Union army and fight to preserve the Union, but he could not leave his mother and sisters in poverty.

Fast Facts

The Civil War

Who: The United States (the Union, or the North) against the Confederate States of America, made up of southern states that had seceded from the Union.

When: April 11, 1861–May 1865

Why: Southern states, believing the election of Abraham Lincoln threatened states' rights and slavery, seceded from the United States and fought for their independence. The North fought to restore the southern states to the Union, and later to end slavery.

Where: States along the border between the Union and the Confederacy, especially Virginia and Tennessee. Confederate forces had some early successes, but were overcome by the Union's superior resources. Major northern victories came at Gettysburg, Pennsylvania, and Vicksburg, Mississippi (both July 1863); Atlanta, Georgia (September 1864); and Petersburg and Richmond, Virginia (both April 1865).

Outcome: The Confederate Army of Northern Virginia surrendered to Union forces April 9, 1865, ending the major fighting. The victorious North passed legislation that abolished slavery, gave civil rights to former slaves, and put defeated states under military rule.

In November 1863, Cleveland gained appointment as assistant district attorney for Erie County, which included Buffalo. He left his law firm and took a pay cut in order to serve as a prosecutor. The district attorney was an elderly man in poor health, so most of the work fell on Cleveland. He presented many cases to grand juries personally, developing work habits that would serve him well throughout his political life. In preparing for a trial, Cleveland painstakingly researched every aspect of the case. He committed his argument to memory, so that he delivered his courtroom speeches flawlessly and without notes. After spending the day in the courtroom, he often worked in his office until two o'clock in the morning.

Meanwhile, the great war dragged on and on. The North had more people and many more resources than the South, but Confederate armies proved difficult to defeat. On March 3, 1863, Congress passed the Conscription Act, designed to draft eligible men for army service. Cleveland's number came up on the day the new act became effective. Luckily for the family, the law allowed men to find and pay a substitute to take their place. Cleveland paid a Polish immigrant named George Benninsky $150 to serve in his place. (Benninsky made it safely through the war, serving mostly in a military hospital in Washington, D.C.)

Private Practice

As the Civil War was finally coming to an end, the Erie County district attorney retired, and Grover Cleveland ran for the office. His Republican opponent was a friend and roommate, Lyman Bass. The Buffalo *Courier* endorsed Cleveland, but he was fighting an uphill battle. Erie County was heavily Republican. In the end, Lyman Bass won the election, and Cleveland lost his position as assistant district attorney to a Republican appointee. There were no hard feelings, however; Cleveland and Bass remained close friends.

Out of office and out of a job, Cleveland began his own private law practice. He went into partnership first with Isaac K. Vanderpoel, and later with Albert

Laning and Oscar Folsom. The partners made good livings from their work, and, Cleveland's reputation as a lawyer continued to climb.

In court, Cleveland was all business, appearing to outsiders as gruff and stiff. Away from work, however, he was a down-to-earth man who spent hours with his friends in local saloons discussing politics over steins of beer and overflowing plates of sausages and sauerkraut. He also enjoyed a friendly game of poker or billiards.

Cleveland walked back and forth from court to his office, and found time for fishing and hunting on weekends. Still, he did not like exercise and spent most of his time sitting down. Since moving to Buffalo, he had put on 100 pounds (45 kilograms). His nieces and nephews affectionately called him "Uncle Jumbo." Cleveland remained a bachelor throughout his Buffalo years. When one of his sisters asked him if he thought about marrying, he answered with a smile, "A good many times; and the more I think of it, the more I think I'll not do it."

Sheriff Cleveland

In 1870, leaders from the Democratic party in Erie County asked Cleveland to run for sheriff. This was an unusual move, since previous sheriffs had been former police officers, not lawyers. Much of the job centered on running the jail. Friends tried to persuade Cleveland not to run, but he decided to give it a try.

When Grover Cleveland arrived in 1855, Buffalo was the second-largest city in New York State with 100,000 people. By 1865, its population had doubled. Many of the newcomers were *immigrants*, people from Germany and Ireland, who had settled in the city.

During the 25 years Cleveland lived in Buffalo, it became a major American city. It was a crossroads between the East and Midwest and between Canada and the United States.

As a growing transportation and manufacturing center, Buffalo was a working-man's town with thousands of dockworkers and factory hands. Along the streets there were saloons at every corner. Dance halls and gambling dens were easy to find. Fights and robberies were common, and in some neighborhoods, police patrolled only in pairs.

Prosperous citizens were beginning to campaign for civic improvement. They complained about the crime rate and about the cloud of factory smoke that often hung over the city. The city had no sewage system and its drinking water was polluted, causing epidemics of disease. City government seemed powerless to improve conditions in the city. Newspapers pointed out that city officials seemed to get rich, but conditions did not improve. Pressure was mounting to change the situation and find a way to address the city's problems. Grover Cleveland was one of the citizens who responded to the call for *reform*.

☆ ★ ☆

The position could easily pay him $40,000 over three years, and he might have more free time to read and study law.

Against strong opposition from the Republican candidate, Cleveland won a close election. He took office on January 1, 1871. At age 33, he was part of a county government notorious for corruption in a city outsiders considered lawless. Could he make a difference?

He began by examining the record of past sheriffs. He learned that the companies that supplied food, firewood, and other supplies to the jail were connected to political leaders and that they were cheating on their deliveries. They billed the county for a large quantity, but delivered only a fraction of that amount. Cleveland began counting each load of wood and each bag of oats in a delivery to make sure he received as much as he paid for. If he got shortchanged, he complained publicly, whether the supplier was a Republican or a Democrat. Cleveland tackled all aspects of his new position, no matter how unpleasant. One of his responsibilities was executing criminals sentenced to death by hanging. He could have paid someone else to carry out the executions, but he himself hanged two convicted murderers.

After a single term as sheriff, Cleveland decided not to run again and returned to private law practice. He set up a partnership with Lyman Bass and

Wilson "Shan" Bissell. Bissell became Cleveland's closest lifelong friend. Cleveland later appointed him U.S. postmaster general.

In 1875, another close friend and former law partner, Oscar Folsom, was thrown from his horse-drawn carriage and killed. The court appointed Cleveland to be administrator of Oscar's estate. Caring greatly for Mrs. Folsom and her eleven-year-old daughter Frances (known as Frank), Cleveland went beyond his legal duties, helping and advising the Folsoms. Frank Folsom would later play an enormous role in his life.

A Reform Mayor

The city of Buffalo could not solve its problems because its government had long been controlled by corrupt politicians. These crooked "bosses" rigged elections, accepted bribes from contractors, and stole money from the city treasury. Reform was sorely needed, and the Democratic committee of Erie County decided that Cleveland was just the man to make it happen. Known as an able and honest lawyer, Cleveland had proven again and again his disdain for crooked politicians. In 1881, the committee asked Cleveland to run for mayor.

Cleveland was reluctant, but finally agreed to run. Later that day, he entered the Democratic convention to a standing ovation. Cleveland campaigned throughout the city. He told the crowds, "Public officials are the trustees of the people." His call for reforms attracted many Republican and independent voters. Together with Democrats, they helped elect him and defeat his Republican opponent. The city was ready for a change.

Cleveland took the oath of office on January 1, 1882, at the age of 44. He immediately put a stop to the custom of city offices closing early, which allowed city employees to work half a day and receive a full day's pay. During his year as mayor, Cleveland saved the city $1 million, and used his *veto* power many times to stop corrupt practices. He was given a new nickname, "Our Veto Mayor."

Shortly after entering office, Cleveland tackled the urgent task of creating a city sewer system. For years, sewage had run into a local canal. It seeped into the drinking water, spreading diseases that had killed hundreds of city residents. Something needed to be done. Year after year, citizens and city officials had argued about a plan, but had gotten nowhere. Cleveland used his stubborn nature to insist that knowledgeable engineers be hired to devise the plan. He demanded action—and clean drinking water for the city's residents. In June he got his way, and the city was on its way to greater health.

June also brought another triumph for the new mayor. When the city council gave a street-cleaning contract to a man who bid five times more than the lowest bidder, Cleveland investigated. He learned that at least $50,000 of the bid was to pay off the dishonest councilmen. Cleveland vetoed the contract. Citizens cheered. Embarrassed by the publicity, the council upheld Cleveland's veto 23 to 2, and gave the street-cleaning contract to the lowest bidder.

About the same time, the Democratic party was choosing its candidate to run for governor of New York State. Democrats from western New York proposed Cleveland. At the nominating convention in September, Cleveland was chosen, supported by enthusiastic delegates from around the state. The people of New York responded to Cleveland's campaign and his reputation for honesty. He was elected by a landslide, gaining nearly 200,000 more votes than his Republican opponent. He was on a fast track to higher office.

Chapter 3

"Bigger and Better" ————————

The government of New York State bubbled with corruption. Reform Democrats hoped that Cleveland could carry out the same cleanup in Albany (the state capital) that he had in Buffalo. Cleveland wanted this, too, but was anxious about his ability to deliver. He wrote to his brother William, "I know that I am honest and sincere in my desire to do well [for the people of the state]; but the question is whether I know enough to accomplish what I desire."

Cleveland was sworn in as governor on New Year's Day 1883. Accompanied by his friend Shan Bissell and political adviser Daniel S. Lamont, he walked through freshly fallen snow to the state capitol to take the oath of office. Awaiting him was an audience bursting with curiosity to see their new, little-known governor. Cleveland gave his inaugural speech without notes. The next day, he gave a more comprehensive address to the *legislature*, the state's lawmaking body. In it he detailed a plan to reform the way state employees were hired. He spoke of a smaller government, getting rid of unnecessary offices, and fairer taxes.

Cleveland opened his office to all. People streamed through the door steadily. Faithful Democrats came expecting government jobs, but Cleveland was

After a term as the reform mayor of Buffalo, Cleveland is sworn in as governor of New York in January 1883.

determined to fill jobs on the basis of merit, not to reward past service to the party. If a person suggested he wanted a political reward for a contribution to the campaign, Cleveland would narrow his eyes to slits and say in an icy voice, "I don't know that I understand you."

Cleveland was also tough on the legislature, studying each bill it passed and refusing to sign those not in the public interest. Between January 26 and March 1, he vetoed eight measures, earning the nickname "Veto Governor." His supporters began calling him "Grover the Good."

In New York City, the Democratic party was dominated by Tammany Hall, a political machine known nationwide for its corrupt practices. The Tammany Hall bosses presented a bill to reduce the fare for New York City's elevated railroads from ten cents to five. The bill was popular, and Cleveland would have been happy to see the fares reduced, but he concluded that the bill broke a legal contract with the railroads' owners. Reluctantly, he vetoed the bill. He said, "By tomorrow at this time I shall be the most unpopular man in the state of New York!" This was the first of many conflicts between Cleveland and Tammany Hall. Cleveland was surprised when many newspapers praised his courage. One of them wrote, "Grover Cleveland has shown himself what we took him on trust to be last fall—bigger and better than his party."

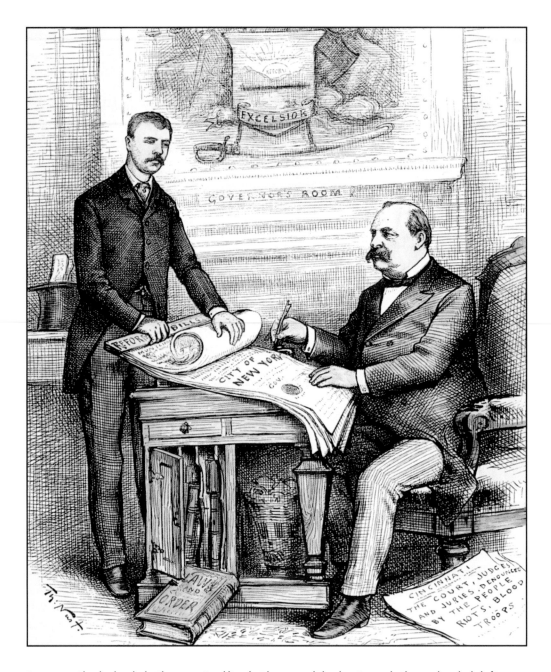

As governor, Cleveland worked with a young Republican legislator named Theodore Roosevelt. The two shared a belief in government reform, and both later served as president.

National Attention

Cleveland continued his practice of long workdays, often beginning at seven o'clock over breakfast and going until late at night. His leisure time was limited, and his tastes remained simple. One of the few changes he made to the governor's mansion was to add a billiard table. He also liked to play cards with his friends on Sunday afternoons. He joked about this, "My father used to say that it was wicked to go fishing on Sunday, but he never said anything about draw-poker."

That fall, Cleveland strongly opposed the reelection of a Democratic state senator named Thomas Grady, who was backed by Tammany Hall. He drafted a letter to Boss Kelly advising him to back another candidate. Hoping to embarrass the governor, Kelly gave the letter to the New York *World*, which published it and criticized Cleveland for meddling in the election. Other newspapers around the country published the letter with a different message. They praised Cleveland for opposing a big-city boss in his own party. For the first time, Cleveland was gaining national attention.

A Public Trust

In 1884, the Republican party *nominated* James G. Blaine as its candidate for president. Blaine was brilliant and charming, and was one of the party's most powerful leaders. Even so, reform-minded Republicans were dismayed because Blaine had

The powerful James G. Blaine gained the Republican nomination for president in 1884.

been involved in corrupt dealings during his long career. A group of reform Republicans refused to support him and soon attracted Democrats and independents favoring government reforms. Newspapers called the group the "Mugwumps," an old Indian word for "chiefs."

The Democratic nominating convention met in Chicago in July. No Democrat had been elected president for 28 years, but it seemed in 1884 that the party might win at last, especially if they nominated a reform candidate. By the time the convention opened, Cleveland had a real chance at the nomination. There had been so much corruption in both political parties in the past 20 years that Cleveland stood out for his honesty and his devotion to reform. Not all Democrats agreed, however. Tammany Hall's John Kelly controlled more than 600 delegates at the convention, and he worked hard to defeat Cleveland's nomination. In the end, Kelly's tough tactics actually helped Cleveland. The chairman of the delegates from Wisconsin announced his state's support of Cleveland, saying, "They love Cleveland for his character, but they love him also for the enemies he has made!" Cleveland won the nomination.

Democrats, seeking a reform candidate, nominated Grover Cleveland, who had made a name for himself as mayor of Buffalo and governor of New York.

Cleveland was at his desk in Albany while the convention met in Chicago. When a cannon was fired outside the Capitol, one of his assistants shouted, "They're firing a salute in your honor, Governor!"

"Do you think so?" Cleveland asked.

A few minutes later the telephone rang, and Cleveland learned the good news. His face brightened, and he said to Lamont, "By Jove, that is something, isn't it?"

Daniel Lamont set to work shaping the campaign. Campaign worker William Hudson boiled down Cleveland's belief that public officials are the trustees of the people into a catchy slogan, "Public office is a public trust." Cleveland agreed to make it his own.

Mudslinging ————————————————————

Ten days after the convention, the Republican Buffalo *Evening Telegraph* dropped a bombshell on Cleveland's campaign. "A TERRIBLE TALE: A DARK CHAPTER IN A PUBLIC MAN'S HISTORY," read the headline. The story reported that Grover Cleveland was the father of a child born years earlier to a Buffalo woman named Maria Halpin. The story called Cleveland "a foe to virtue, an enemy of the family."

When party officials asked how they should respond, Cleveland replied, "Whatever you do, tell the truth." He said that he had been a friend of Maria Halpin in the 1870s, that she had given birth to a child, and that he had agreed to provide for the baby until it could be adopted. Investigators found the truth was as Cleveland had told it. Republicans kept the scandal in front of the public throughout the campaign. One famous jingle was familiar to voters from coast to coast:

Ma! Ma! Where's my Pa?

Gone to the White House. Ha! Ha! Ha!

Behind the headlines, there was a more complicated story. During the early 1870s, two of Cleveland's friends had also spent time with Maria Halpin. She named the child Oscar Folsom Cleveland, using Cleveland's last name, but also that of Oscar Folsom, Cleveland's law partner and friend. Since Folsom was married, Cleveland may have agreed to claim fatherhood to save his partner's family from scandal. Cleveland did not comment on this part of the story, and no one knows who the actual father was. Cleveland's involvement in the Maria Halpin affair did not improve his reputation. Because he told the truth, however, many voters forgave him and gave him credit for facing up to the charges.

Some Democrats and Mugwumps also made scandalous accusations against Blaine. They claimed that in 1876 Blaine took a bribe from a railroad company, then used his influence in Congress to get favors for the railroad. Blaine had sent a confidential letter to a middleman for the railroad which included the words, "Burn this letter." The letter fell into the hands of Blaine's enemies and appeared in newspapers across the country. Soon Cleveland supporters were chanting, "Burn this letter! Burn this letter!" At a parade in New York, supporters burned a huge imitation of the letter, and chanted:

Blaine, Blaine, James G. Blaine,

The continental liar from the State of Maine.

As the campaign came down to the last week, it was too close to predict. Then, on October 29, James Blaine made a serious mistake. That morning he appeared at a gathering of New York clergymen who had met to endorse him. A Presbyterian minister named Samuel Burchard greeted Blaine with a speech in which he characterized Democrats as the party with a heritage of "Rum, Romanism, and Rebellion." This suggested that Democrats were drinkers of alcohol, Roman Catholics, or southerners whose rebellion caused the Civil War.

This ugly remark went unnoticed by Blaine, who may not have been listening. A supporter of Cleveland did notice it and made sure it was reprinted in

Political cartoonist Thomas Nast supported Cleveland for president. Here he ridicules the Republican candidate Blaine as a "magnetic man" who attracts scandals instead of votes.

newspapers across the country. The next day, Blaine disavowed the remark, but the damage was done. To win New York State, he needed the votes of the huge population of Irish and German Roman Catholics in New York City. The slighting reference to "Rum and Romanism" caused many of them to vote for Cleveland instead. Their votes helped decide the election.

Governor Cleveland receives election results in the governor's office. The election was so close that the outcome was not certain for three days. Cleveland gained the victory, becoming the first Democrat elected president in 28 years.

Victory

Election day arrived in upstate New York with gusts of cold, driving rain. Cleveland traveled home to Buffalo to cast his vote in the election. Soon afterward, he took the train back to Albany to await the results. He didn't need to hurry. The election was so close that the outcome was not clear for three days. In the end, he carried New York State by a narrow margin, and his home-state victory helped him win the presidency.

Cleveland gained only 22,000 votes more than James G. Blaine, one of the smallest victory margins in history. He won New York by less than 150 votes out of more than a million. In the electoral college, where the final decision is made, Cleveland won 219 votes to Blaine's 182.

Cleveland was the first Democratic president elected since 1856. Celebrations erupted around the country. The president-elect, however, looked forward with a sober sense of duty. He wrote to his friend Shan Bissell, "I look upon the four years next to come as a dreadful self-inflicted penance for the good of my country. I can see no pleasure in it and no satisfaction, only a hope that I may be of service to my people."

Chapter 4

What a Day!

People perched on windowsills. Some balanced high atop tree branches. Thousands jostled for position on the grounds of the Capitol, swaying in time to the cheerful brass-band music. More than 250,000 people streamed into Washington, D.C., from across the land, sleeping in hallways when the hotels ran out of rooms. All wanted to be a part of this momentous occasion: the first *inauguration* of a Democratic president since before the Civil War.

Suddenly a wild cheer erupted from the sea of black-hatted spectators. The man of the hour had arrived. Curious onlookers squinted into the brilliant sunshine of that March morning to catch a glimpse of the new president. In those days before radio or television, most had never seen him or heard his voice.

Grover Cleveland, resplendent in a long, double-breasted black coat and gray striped pants, removed his hat, smoothed his hair,

Democratic supporters filled Washington for Cleveland's inauguration. That night there was a huge fireworks display near the recently completed Washington Monument.

and launched into his address. His resonant voice rang over the crowd. As usual, he delivered the entire speech flawlessly without notes. After the address, Cleveland took the oath of office, placing his hand on his own personal Bible, a cherished gift from his mother.

A Flurry

Cleveland settled into the White House with his staff, including his trusted private secretary Dan Lamont. The staff was so small that sometimes Cleveland himself answered the one White House telephone. At times he even opened the front door when someone knocked. Still a bachelor, Cleveland asked Rose, his youngest sister, to act as the White House hostess. An ardent feminist, Rose was intelligent and well educated. She admitted later that shaking hands with people in long reception lines was so boring that she sometimes mentally reviewed Greek verbs.

To find his own peace of mind, Cleveland liked going alone to the White House conservatory to admire the flowers. He also enjoyed frequent visits from his brothers and sisters and their families. "Uncle Jumbo" wanted his nieces and nephews around him as much as possible. One thing he wasn't particularly fond of was the cooking of the White House's French chef. He wrote to a friend, "I must go to dinner. I wish it was to eat a pickled herring, Swiss cheese, and a chop instead of the French stuff I shall find."

DANIEL WEBSTER.

All who favored political reform were hopeful when Cleveland took office.

Like the presidents before him, he was besieged by office seekers. The federal government had 110,000 jobs that the president had the duty to fill. Ambitious men (especially Democrats) who wanted one of these positions felt free to visit him at the White House to make their case. People accosted the president day and night, begging for jobs. He was grateful to Democrats who helped elect him, but he was determined to appoint people who were well qualified for their jobs. Still, he complained to the White House doctor, "Those office-seekers. They haunt me in my dreams!"

Silver and Gold

When Cleveland entered the White House, presidents were not nearly as powerful as they became in later years. Congress took charge of the country's business and believed that the chief executive's main job was to carry out the laws that Congress had passed. As a reform-minded mayor and governor, Cleveland had learned to take a strong hand in making government policy. It is not surprising that he soon came into conflict with Congress.

The first major issue involved the country's money. Like major European nations, the United States was on the gold standard. Its paper money and coins could be exchanged for gold. A powerful faction in the U.S. Congress was in favor of backing the dollar with gold *and* silver. Silver mines in the western states and territories were producing huge quantities of the metal. Mine owners hoped that the government would buy much of their production to help support the currency. Political leaders believed that using silver could help increase the supply of money, making it easier for businesses and individuals to borrow money. Seven years earlier, in 1878, backers of silver had succeeded in passing the Bland-Allison Act. The act required the U.S. Treasury to buy between $2 million and $4 million of silver each month.

Cleveland opposed making silver one of the standards for currency. He insisted that the dollar's value should be based only on gold. In fact, the Bland-Allison bill was causing serious damage to government finances. Foreign nations and large U.S. businesses insisted on being paid in gold, reducing the government's supply.

With the support of a few congressional leaders, Cleveland sent a message to Congress in December 1885, calling for the *repeal* (cancellation) of the Bland-Allison Act. Bankers and leading businessmen were encouraged. They expected Cleveland to use his influence to repeal the bill, but he soon announced that he would stay out of the debate. Silver supporters were thrilled. A New York *Herald* headline shouted, "DEMOCRATS WITHOUT A LEADER." The forces favoring silver defeated the repeal. Cleveland's failure to lead the fight for repeal proved to be one of the major mistakes in his presidency.

In 1885, Apaches in the Southwest revolted against living on government-supervised reservations. Led by their chiefs Geronimo and Natchez (on horseback), they began the last major Indian war, but were soon subdued by military force.

Pension Problems

In the years after the Civil War, the federal government took action to provide assistance for veterans who fought for the Union. Surviving veterans received government *pensions*, payments based on their injuries and length of service. Families of Union fighters killed in action also received support. Veterans' organizations persuaded Congress to broaden the benefit programs and give individuals whose applications were turned down the right to appeal. If a veteran's claim was rejected by the government Pension Bureau, he also had the right to appeal the matter to his local congressman. The congressman then presented a "private bill" to Congress asking that the pension be granted. Congress approved thousands of these private bills without studying them closely and sent them to the president to sign into law. By the spring of 1886, Cleveland's office was filled with these private bills for his approval.

Some of the appeals were justified, but hundreds of others stretched the pension law to the breaking point. One person wanted a pension for an ankle he'd broken *before* he entered military service. Another sought money for injuries he'd gotten from the explosion of a Fourth of July cannon at his home. Unlike earlier presidents, Cleveland studied each bill carefully. He judged each case without regard to party, signing the honest ones and vetoing those that were fraudulent. Civil War pensions were one of the largest items in the federal budget. Cleveland saw the dishonest appeals as theft from the government and an insult to all the veterans who deserved government benefits for their service.

Cleveland's vetoes enraged congressmen who had sponsored the bills and caused widespread anger among Civil War veterans. Cleveland was the first president elected since the war who had not served in the Union army, and veterans thought he lacked appreciation for their services. Powerful veterans' organizations would remember the vetoes when Cleveland came up for reelection.

The Haymarket Riot

Veterans' pensions were not the only emotional issue in 1886. The conflict between workers and management was growing more dangerous by the day. Workers were organizing into *labor unions*, which could negotiate for better wages and benefits with employers. If the workers felt they were treated unfairly, they would *strike*, walking off their jobs until a fair agreement could be reached. Owners of factories and mills did not recognize the right of workers to organize and bargain for their wages. Owners reasoned that since they owned the factories and equipment, bought the raw materials, and took all the business risks, they had the right to set workers' wages and work rules without negotiation.

In the spring of 1886, workers at the McCormick Reaper Company near Chicago went out on strike. During a clash with police, one of the strikers was killed. A group of *anarchists* (believers in doing away with governments) who supported the strike called a rally in Chicago's Haymarket Square. The speakers addressed a crowd of about 1,500, and police officers stood at the edges to prevent violence. About 10 p.m., rain began to fall and the crowd started to drift off. Just as the speaker said, "We're peaceable," someone threw a homemade bomb into a cluster of policemen. Seven officers were killed, and others began firing into the crowd. No one knows how many were killed and wounded that night.

During a strike in Chicago, strike leaders and anarchists held a rally at Haymarket Square. Just as it was ending, someone threw a bomb into a group of policemen. The blast killed several officers and set off a battle in which many were killed and injured.

Cleveland took no action in the Haymarket attack, but he was troubled by the conflict between labor and management. With millions now at work in factories, he believed that the grievances of workers deserved attention. Nearly a year later, on April 22, 1887, he became the first president to address Congress on the issue of labor. He declared that the value of laborers to the country's prosperity should be recognized and that "the welfare of the laboring man" should be a concern of the government. He later signed a bill into law that made national trade unions legal.

White House Wedding

In the meantime, there were also momentous events in Grover Cleveland's personal life. On May 29, 1886, Grover Cleveland personally sent notes to close friends and family, announcing some happy news.

> I am to be married on Wednesday evening at seven o'clock at the White House to Miss Folsom. It will be a very quiet affair and I will be extremely grateful at your attendance on the occasion.
>
> Yours Sincerely,
>
> Grover Cleveland

Miss Folsom was young Frances "Frankie" Folsom, the daughter of Cleveland's old Buffalo law partner and friend. She was now a beautiful, intelligent young woman, 21 years old. Frankie and her mother had visited Cleveland when he was governor in New York, and since then he had been writing to her. He proposed to her in 1885, and she accepted. Only close friends and family knew about the engagement, and they kept it quiet for nearly a year. The White House finally announced the engagement on May 28, 1886.

Frances Folsom, known to her friends as Frankie, was 21 years old when she married Grover Cleveland in 1886. Cleveland was 49.

The wedding caused a public sensation. Frances would become the youngest first lady in history, and the wedding marked the first time a president had been married in the White House. Thousands crowded onto the White House lawns hoping to catch a glimpse of the happy couple. At 7:00 p.m., bandleader John Philip Sousa gave the signal and the U.S. Marine Band struck up "The

Wedding March." Grover and Frances slowly descended the grand staircase together into the Blue Room, Frank's train trailing gracefully behind her. Roses and pansies covered the room, and two candelabra cast flickering, romantic light on the couple as they exchanged their vows. At Cleveland's insistence, the word "obey" was cut from the wedding vows; instead Frances promised to "love, honor, and keep" her new husband.

As the ceremony ended, church bells tolled across the city and a 21-gun salute boomed from the Navy Yard, causing the swarms of people on the White House lawns to send up a whoop. After a reception and formal dinner with their guests, the couple changed out of their wedding outfits and left the White House under the concealment of tent canvas. A waiting carriage whisked them past cheering crowds lining Pennsylvania Avenue to a special two-car train that took them to Deer Park, a cottage resort in the mountains of western Maryland, for their six-day honeymoon.

Americans adored Frances Folsom Cleveland. Women styled their hair "à la Cleveland" and posed for photos tilting their heads the way she did. The country wanted to know every tidbit about this striking woman. Advertisers put Frank's image on products and advertisements ranging from soaps to cigars—all without permission. Cleveland was furious and asked Congress to pass a bill

The Clevelands were married in the Blue Room of the White House. Guests included family, close friends, and cabinet members and their wives.

making it illegal to use an image of a president's female relative without written consent. The bill didn't pass.

After his marriage, President Cleveland seemed more cheerful and outgoing. Frances was fond of social life, and was soon serving as hostess at dazzling dinner parties and dances in the White House. Cleveland was happy to work in the mansion and to participate in his new wife's entertainments, but he was less happy about living there. He bought a large house on 23 acres (9 hectares) just north of Washington where he and Frances spent much of their spare time. The house had sweeping views of the Potomac River and the city of Washington. Before long, it became a small farm, with a cow, chickens, ducks, and numerous dogs.

Railroads and Farmers

The most powerful business in the United States at this time was the railroads. Rail lines crisscrossed the country and had taken over the job of transporting raw materials and manufactured goods. They also transported grain, livestock, and other farm products from far-flung farming regions to growing towns and cities.

As the railroads increased their charges for hauling goods, farmers were the first to be squeezed. They complained that they were charged more for shipping than mining companies that shipped coal and iron. Sometimes the freight charges were higher than the cost of growing the crops. Railroads insisted on

The Statue of Liberty, a gift to the United States from France, was dedicated by President Cleveland on October 28, 1886. That night, fireworks lit up New York Bay as hundreds of ships and small craft sailed past for a closer look.

The fall after his wedding, Grover Cleveland presided at the dedication of the Statue of Liberty on an island in New York Harbor. A gift from the people of France, the statue had been nearly 22 years in the making. Schoolchildren in the United States contributed their pennies to help pay for the huge pedestal on which the statue was placed.

The dedication day, October 28, 1886, was dismal and rainy, but more than a million people gathered along the shores of Manhattan, Brooklyn, and Staten Island to see the statue unveiled. Thousands of boats crammed the harbor. President Cleveland presided over the noisy ceremony, which was filled with speeches, 21-gun salutes, and rollicking brass-band refrains. More than a century later, millions still arrive each year to view the statue, which has become a symbol of the country's liberties and her hospitality.

☆ ★ ☆

their right to charge whatever rate they chose. Farm states pressured Congress to do something to ensure that the railroads charged customers fairly. President Cleveland supported a bill to establish the Interstate Commerce Commission to review railroad rates, and in February 1887, he signed it into law. This was a first step by the federal government in regulating powerful business enterprises.

One Nation

Even though the Civil War had ended more than 20 years earlier, conflicts and resentments between North and South still troubled the nation. President Cleveland's Democratic party was the majority party throughout the South. As the first Democrat elected president since the war, he was determined to help reunify the country. In 1887, he and Frances set out on a long tour of the West and the South, giving the American public an opportunity to get to know their president better. They visited 18 states, and Cleveland addressed dozens of speeches to enthusiastic crowds, receiving an especially warm welcome in states of the old Confederacy.

Great Tariff Debate

Upon returning from his trip, Cleveland addressed one of the most controversial issues of the day—tariffs. For more than 50 years, the major parties in the United

States had divided on this issue. A *tariff* is a tax charged on goods imported into a country from other countries. The tariff had two purposes. One was to raise money for the operation of the federal government. The second was to protect U.S. businesses against foreign competition. Tariffs made foreign-made goods more expensive, encouraging U.S. consumers to buy goods made at home.

The Republican party was strongly in favor of high "protective" tariffs. Most in Cleveland's Democratic party favored lower tariffs. They claimed that high tariffs increased prices on goods that everyone needs, making it more difficult for ordinary people to afford many items. Cleveland also favored lower tariffs, and he saw an opportunity to persuade Congress to lower them. High tariffs had brought the federal government more money than it could spend, and it had a large surplus.

Cleveland urged Congress to review tariff rates and lower them. Cleveland's advisers warned him that a stand for low tariffs could cost him the next election, but he rejected the advice. He said to a friend, "What is the use of being elected or reelected unless you stand for something?"

In a historic annual address to Congress on December 6, 1887, Cleveland discussed only one issue: lower tariffs. He urged that the cuts be made not on luxury items, but on necessities such as sugar, coffee, and cloth. The press praised the president for addressing this controversial issue.

Once again, Cleveland did not follow up his recommendations by working to gain support among his friends in Congress. The so-called Great Tariff Debate began in the House on April 17. A bill passed in the House with a narrow margin on July 21, but the Senate, controlled by high-tariff Republicans, blocked the bill. The deadlock in Congress made the tariff the big issue in the presidential campaign that fall.

Drooping Canvass

Prior to Cleveland's bold stand on the tariff, he was practically guaranteed reelection. But by the end of 1887, he had managed to offend many Americans. Veterans were angry that he had vetoed hundreds of private pension bills. Factory owners were angry about his support for lower tariffs. Most of the angry people were Republicans.

Cleveland easily won the Democratic nomination for reelection. The Republicans nominated Benjamin Harrison, who had been a senator from Indiana and was the grandson of former president William Henry Harrison. Harrison had a cold personality, but he was a shrewd politician, and he had the support of an experienced Republican campaign staff. Republicans swamped the country with flyers and speeches, newspaper ads and pamphlets. Many warned workers that

Benjamin Harrison of Indiana became the Republican candidate for president in 1888. He promised a return to high tariffs to protect U.S. businesses and more support for Civil War veterans.

lower tariffs would flood the country with foreign goods and cause many to lose their jobs.

The Democratic campaign was less aggressive. As before, Cleveland stayed at his desk attending to business, and his campaign managers seemed to lack enthusiasm. The New York *Herald* reported, "The Republicans began with an aggressive campaign and are forcing the fighting in every state. . . . While the Republican canvass shows animation the Democratic canvass droops and hangs."

On election night, Cleveland waited for the returns in the White House library with Frank and a few friends. At midnight, Navy Secretary William Whitney came from the telegraph room. "Well, it's all up," he said. Cleveland actually won 100,000 more popular votes than Harrison, but lost in the electoral college vote, 233 to 168. Disappointed

After defeating Cleveland in a close election, Harrison (with white beard) took the oath office on a cold, rainy day. Grover Cleveland stands to the left of Harrison.

Democrats suggested that Republicans had bought or stolen votes in Indiana and New York, which Harrison won by very small margins.

When a friend mentioned that he probably lost the election because of his stand on tariffs, Cleveland said, "Perhaps I made a mistake from the party standpoint; but damn it, it was right. I have at least that satisfaction."

On Harrison's inauguration day a steady rain pelted down. In a show of friendship, Cleveland held an umbrella over Harrison's head as he gave his speech. After Cleveland left with Harrison for the ceremony, Frances said goodbye to the White House staff. To one White House staff member she said, "Now, Jerry, I want you to take good care of all the furniture and ornaments in the house and not let any of them get lost or broken, for I want to find everything just as it is now, when we come back again."

Jerry, not sure what she meant, asked when that might be.

She smiled, and answered: "We are coming back just four years from today."

Chapter 5

Happy Days

Several weeks after leaving the White House, Cleveland wrote to his friend Shan Bissell, "I feel that I am fast taking the place which I desire to reach—the place of a respectable private citizen."

The Clevelands decided to settle in New York City. Cleveland became an associate with a prestigious law firm and bought a handsome four-story brownstone on fashionable Madison Avenue. He could walk to or from his office. Occasionally, the Clevelands attended a play. More often they entertained friends at home.

During their first summer, they visited Cape Cod, Massachusetts, and fell in love with the area. In 1891, they bought a clapboard cottage overlooking the water, and named it Gray Gables. Cleveland recalled the summers spent at Gray Gables as some of the happiest times of his life. He was able to fish to his heart's content, and enjoyed repairing the neighborhood children's toys or whittling a special gift for one of them.

A Return to Public Life

Cleveland found it easy enough to stay out of politics for a time. Before long, however, he began to notice what the Harrison administration was doing in Washington. The Republicans had taken the opportunity to raise tariffs, and Congress was spending huge amounts on wasteful and inappropriate projects. In December 1889, Congress passed the Sherman Silver Purchase Act, a bill that increased the amount of silver the government was required to buy, and was trying to pass a bill authorizing unlimited coinage of silver.

When Cleveland expressed his dismay, his advisers warned him that speaking out against silver could ruin his chance for reelection. He dismissed the warning. "I am supposed to be a leader of my party," he said. "If any word of mine can check these dangerous fallacies, it is my duty to give that word, whatever the cost may be to me."

He wrote a strongly worded article that became known as "The Silver Letter," which appeared in newspapers across the country. He predicted disaster if "we enter upon the dangerous and reckless experiment of free, unlimited, and independent silver coinage." To his delight, the silver coinage bill failed to pass. Cleveland's supporters took the letter as a sign he was ready to run for president again.

Another delight came on October 3, 1891. Frances Cleveland gave birth to the couple's first child, a daughter they named Ruth.

The Clevelands welcomed their first child, who became known as "Baby Ruth," in 1891.

"No Secret Promises"

Cleveland's supporters began a campaign to nominate him for president in 1892. Once again, his enemies in New York City's Tammany Hall worked to prevent the nomination, but with little effect. On June 22, at the National Democratic Convention in Chicago, Democrats rallied around Cleveland. The Republicans nominated Benjamin Harrison for a second term. He had made many enemies during his term, however, and Democrats were hopeful that Cleveland could oust him from the White House. This would be the only race in U.S. history between two major candidates who had both served as president.

This Democratic campaign had strong leadership. Cleveland disagreed with it only on strategy for winning New York State. The campaign manager thought Cleveland should make peace with Tammany Hall and finally convinced him to attend a dinner with important Tammany chiefs. After the meal, they promised Cleveland their support—if he promised them favors in return. Cleveland angrily slammed his meaty fist on the table, and said, "Gentlemen, I will not go into the White House pledged to you or to anyone else. I will make no secret promises. I'll be damned if I will!"

The campaign of 1892 was a quiet one. Late that summer, President Harrison's wife became seriously ill with tuberculosis. Harrison gave up campaigning to be at her side, and out of respect, Cleveland curtailed his own

In 1892, Cleveland was nominated for a third time to run for president. His vice presidential running mate was Adlai E. Stevenson of Illinois.

campaigning. On October 25, less than two weeks before the election, Carrie Harrison died.

On election day, voters swept Grover Cleveland back into office. This time, he won by a healthy margin, gaining nearly 500,000 more votes than Harrison and winning in the electoral college, 277 to 145. He won such

The Homestead Strike of 1892

During the summer of 1892, labor conflict was once again in the headlines. This time, workers went on strike at the Carnegie Steel Works in Homestead, Pennsylvania, near Pittsburgh, when the company announced wage reductions. The plant owner, Andrew Carnegie, was one of the wealthiest and most famous business leaders of the time. His manager responded with a *lockout*, keeping union workers out of the plant and hiring nonunion workers to take their place.

To guard the strikebreakers and the plant, the Carnegie plant hired 300 men from the Pinkerton Detective Agency. When the Pinkerton men arrived at the mill on barges early on July 6, they were met by 5,000 angry union members and their supporters, including women brandishing clubs. Shots were fired by both sides, and the Pinkerton men surrendered. When the smoke cleared, ten people had been killed (five from each side) and more than 60 were wounded. Although the union supporters won the first battle, they lost the war. Pennsylvania Governor Robert E. Pattison ordered 8,000 troops from the state militia to guard the plant and the strikebreakers. Union members, left without work, slowly starved.

A few weeks after the violence, Grover Cleveland appeared in New York City's Madison Square Garden to accept his nomination as president. In his only major campaign speech, he expressed outrage at the violence that had erupted at the Homestead Strike and criticized the plant owner's shabby treatment of his laborers. Republicans often defended factory owners and condemned the union members. In the November election, Cleveland gained the support of many workers.

☆ ★ ☆

During the presidential campaign in 1892, violence broke out during a strike against the Carnegie Steel plant in Homestead, Pennsylvania. President Harrison's support of the plant managers over the strikers may have contributed to his defeat by Grover Cleveland in the fall elections.

Republican strongholds as Illinois, Wisconsin, California, and even Harrison's home state of Indiana. At a joyful celebration in New York, Cleveland accepted the results solemnly. He said, "We must hear, above victorious shouts, the call of our fellow countrymen to public duty, and we must put on a garb befitting public servants."

Troubles

Just as Frances had predicted, the Clevelands had returned to the White House. They found some changes there. The old gaslights had been replaced by electric ones. Now, instead of one telephone, there were telephones on many desks, and calls were directed by a full-time switchboard operator.

Things had changed in the country as well. When Cleveland left office after his first term, the federal treasury had a surplus. Now, after the spending of the "billion-dollar Congress," the treasury was nearly empty. The Sherman Silver Purchase Act required the government to use its small gold reserves to buy silver from mines in the West. Bankers warned that the shortage of gold might cause a financial panic.

On May 4, one of the most stable companies in the country, the National Cordage Company, went bankrupt. In the next few days, the prices of stock in other companies took a nosedive. Railroads, which had been borrowing huge sums to build new lines to compete against other railroads, were especially hard hit. Within a month, one railroad company in four had failed. By the middle of August, some 2 million people, nearly 15 percent of the nation's industrial work-force, would be unemployed. The country was heading into the most severe depression it had ever seen.

Cleveland's advisers urged him to call a special session of Congress to repeal the Sherman Silver Purchase Act and take other steps to address the panic. Cleveland agreed, and on June 30, he called a special session of Congress for August 7.

In the meantime, Cleveland was facing a serious threat to his health. In May he first noticed a painful swelling on the roof of his mouth. In the following weeks, the swelling was identified as a cancerous growth. His doctors urged him to have it surgically removed immediately. He had hoped to put off the operation until Congress met, but on June 30, soon after calling the special session, he left the capital for New York. There he boarded the yacht *Oneida*, and the following morning, surgeons operated in secrecy.

The operation, which took only 31 minutes, was a success. When the boat docked at Gray Gables, the Cleveland vacation house on Cape Cod, Frances and young Ruth awaited him. Cleveland walked off the boat and up to the house with-out help. Still, the operation left the president with a huge gap in his mouth which changed the shape of his face and made it difficult for him to speak clearly. He could not appear in public until he was fitted with a rubber replacement for the lost bone. A second operation took place two weeks later. The rubber implant was so well made that his face now looked exactly as it always had. Soon he was speaking as clearly as ever. He remained at Gray Gables for the rest of July, steadily improving.

Reporters were curious. Where had the president been for so long, they asked? His spokesman "confessed" that Cleveland had had two teeth pulled, but said no more. One reporter stumbled on part of the real story, but when he published it, readers refused to take it seriously. The story faded away, and details were not published until 25 years later, after Cleveland's death.

The "Cleveland Depression"

Cleveland returned to Washington in time for the special session of Congress in August. This time, he and his aides did follow through. They spoke individually to each member, insisting that the Sherman Silver Purchase Act must be repealed. The silver supporters had enthusiasm, but they lacked organization. On August 28, the House voted overwhelmingly for repeal. After two more months of tense debate, the Senate too voted for repeal. Grover Cleveland had won a remarkable victory. It was the high point of his second presidency.

Unfortunately, the repeal didn't end the depression. Gold continued to drain from the already low treasury. Cleveland's next step was to issue government *bonds*, borrowing money from private investors in return for a promise to repay the debt with interest at a later time. Four such bond issues provided much-needed gold reserves, but did not bring back prosperity or jobs. They also deeply angered supporters of silver, who began calling the hard times "the Cleveland Depression."

Only months after Cleveland took office in 1893, the stock market crashed, beginning a long, painful depression. Millions were soon unemployed and many became homeless, living in shantytowns like this one in Chicago.

Investors mobbed banks to get their money out before the banks failed.

Mongrel Bill

Cleveland and his advisers believed that high tariffs were one of the causes of the panic of 1893. Once again, he set out to reduce tariffs and encourage free trade, which might bring down prices on many necessities. He collaborated with West Virginia congressman William L. Wilson to draft the bill. It passed the House, but the Senate Finance Committee held it up for five months during 1894. The senators added more than 600 amendments to the bill, changing it completely and actually raising tariffs on some items. Cleveland criticized the bill, but the Senate passed it anyway. Cleveland knew that he could never pass a stronger bill. He decided not to veto the "mongrel bill," but to express his displeasure, he let it pass without his signature. He thought the new tariffs were a small improvement, but still considered the bill a painful defeat.

The Pullman Strike

As economic conditions worsened, businesses cut back, laying off many workers and reducing salaries. The Pullman Palace Car Company near Chicago manufactured luxurious sleeping cars for long-distance rail travelers. The owner, George Pullman, had built solid houses for his workers and had provided them with other uncommon benefits. Now, however, he slashed workers' wages. In May 1894, a

Coxey's Army

On May 1, 1894, a ragtag group of 400 arrived in Washington, D.C. They had been walking for over a month, all the way from Massillon, Ohio. Led by Jacob Coxey, a small businessman who had been forced to lay off all his workers, the men wanted to bring national attention to the plight of the working class. They left Ohio on March 25 and picked up followers along the way. Journalists called the marchers "Coxey's Army." As the march wore on, many marchers fell by the wayside with blistered feet. Others were tired of sleeping on the ground and accepting handouts to eat. By the time they reached Washington, Coxey's men were hugely outnumbered by the spectators who had gathered, and by armed policemen.

A weary Coxey walked onto the Capitol lawn to read his proposal for helping workers out of the depression. He was seized by a swarm of police officers and arrested for walking on the grass. He was jailed for 20 days. Coxey's men finally broke up and found their way back home. As the depression deepened, they continued to symbolize the desperate mood of the unemployed.

Jacob Coxey assembled a group of unemployed men in Ohio and led them on a march to Washington, D.C., to demand help from the government. At left, "Coxey's Army" passes through a small town on the way. At right, Coxey looks through the bars of a Washington jail, where he was imprisoned for trespassing—walking on the grass near the Capitol.

committee of workers from the American Railway Union (ARU) asked Pullman to reduce the high rents on the houses, which the company required the workers to live in. Pullman refused and promptly fired three committee members. A few days later, the vast majority of workers went out on strike. To punish the union, Pullman fired even the workers who refused to strike.

The national leader of the ARU was a prominent young labor leader named Eugene Debs. Debs demanded that Pullman negotiate with him. When Pullman refused, the national ARU voted to strike against all Pullman railcars starting June 26, refusing to run trains that included Pullman cars or services. The strike shut down railroads all across the Midwest. Within days, 20,000 workers walked off of railroad jobs in Chicago, and 40,000 more struck farther west. Mail service was blocked, and passenger and freight trains stopped on the tracks. Wild newspaper accounts made the situation worse. The Chicago *Tribune* ran a headline reading, "THE MOB IS IN CONTROL." Citizens feared a civil war.

Cleveland's attorney general, the government's leading law enforcement official, was a former lawyer for railroad owners. He convinced Cleveland that strong action was needed. Cleveland agreed that the government must keep the mail moving, but still hoped to avoid sending federal troops. The attorney general insisted that there was no other choice, and Cleveland gave in. Troops arrived in Chicago on July 4.

In 1894, railroad workers called a general strike that brought rail travel to a standstill. Strikers wrecked cars, then sent an unmanned locomotive into the cars at high speed.

Soon skirmishes broke out between the strikers and the troops. Seven men were killed, and hundreds were injured. Debs was arrested, and the strike collapsed. In the weeks following the intervention, Cleveland's popularity soared.

President Cleveland sent U.S. troops to help end the strike. This infantry company is patrolling tracks on the Rock Island Railroad.

Many citizens praised Cleveland for his handling of the situation. But champions of labor and of states' rights did not approve. Many historians say he acted too fast, trusting the word of his attorney general over his own judgment.

Hawaii

While economic difficulties continued, Cleveland also attended to situations overseas. Shortly after taking office in 1893, Cleveland set about to mend a situation he found morally atrocious. A few months earlier, a group of American plantation owners in Hawaii had tried to take political control of the Hawaiian Islands. With the help of President Harrison's consul in Hawaii, John L. Stevens, they *deposed* Hawaii's Queen Liliuokalani, removing her as head of the government. U.S. Marines seized government buildings and claimed Hawaii as a U.S. protectorate. American armed forces had helped overthrow a friendly country's government without provocation. Plantation owner Sanford Dole became president of the islands. Harrison immediately sent a treaty to the Senate to *annex* Hawaii, making it a territory of the United States, but Congress refused to approve it. When Cleveland took office, he withdrew the treaty and renounced annexation, but he could not force the new government to return the queen to power. After Cleveland left office, the new administration annexed Hawaii as a territory of the United States.

Disheartened

As Cleveland's second term came to a close, public opinion seemed to turn against him. As Democrats joined the free-silver movement, he had little support,

The States During the Presidency of Grover Cleveland

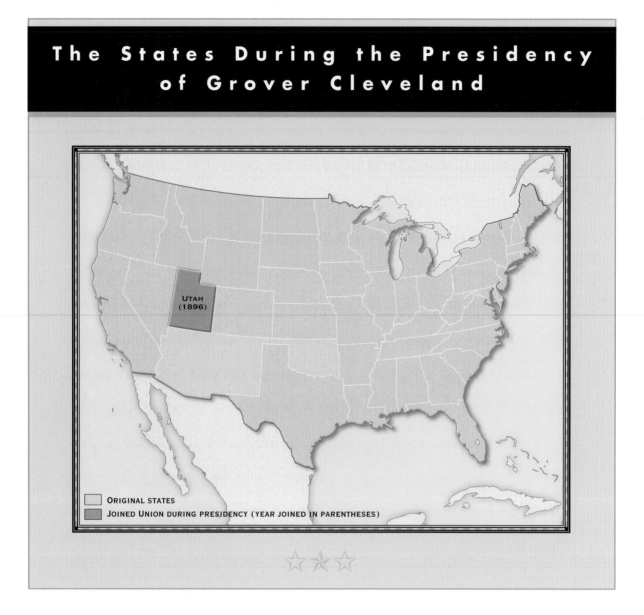

UTAH
(1896)

ORIGINAL STATES

JOINED UNION DURING PRESIDENCY (YEAR JOINED IN PARENTHESES)

even in his own party. Republicans had many reasons to dislike and oppose him. Worst of all, the public continued to blame him for the long-lasting depression which was causing so much distress across the country. One sympathetic newspaper wrote, "No president was ever so persistently and malignantly lied about as Grover Cleveland has been."

In June 1896, the Democratic National Convention met in Chicago to nominate its next presidential candidate. Cleveland made no run for the office, and would not have succeeded in any case. The streets were filled with Democrats from the West and the South wearing badges and carrying banners supporting silver. The party was swinging to support of silver, hoping to increase the money supply and stimulate business activity to end the depression. The party nominated 36-year-old William Jennings Bryan of Nebraska, the youngest presidential candidate of a major party in U.S. history. He was a spellbinding speaker who brought the convention to its feet with his acceptance speech. "You shall not press down upon the brow of labor this crown of thorns—" he shouted, "you shall not crucify mankind upon a cross of gold!"

Cleveland was disappointed and disgusted by the choice of Bryan. He found little to like about the Republican nominee, William McKinley, except that he favored the gold standard. Cleveland privately believed McKinley would make a better president. Publicly, he supported and voted for the Democratic slate.

William McKinley, the winner of the 1896 election, is sworn in as president in March 1897. Outgoing president Cleveland looks on.

McKinley won the election by more than 600,000 votes. The Democrats had lost, but Cleveland's long campaign for keeping the gold standard had won. In fact, the Baltimore *Evening Sun* wrote, "This is Cleveland's day, the vindication of his course."

Still, Cleveland left office despised by many Americans, and he felt utterly disheartened. During a last walk through the White House, he came upon a portrait of himself and asked a staff member to remove it. When asked why, he said he saw "no reason to impose my image on the new president."

Chapter 6

Retirement ———————————————

The Clevelands agreed on settling in Princeton, New Jersey. After the election of 1896, they had visited the university town halfway between New York City and Philadelphia. Later, Frances picked out a large colonial house near the campus of Princeton University, and Cleveland named it Westland, in honor of his friend on the Princeton faculty, Andrew West.

Cleveland worked in the mornings, then walked to the village post office to pick up the mail. In the afternoons, he and Frances might take a ride in their horse-drawn coach, watch their children ride their ponies, or go fishing at a local pond. In the evening, they often entertained friends at dinner. On autumn football afternoons, the Clevelands could be found in their reserved seats at Princeton's Brokaw Field.

Cleveland made a number of good friends with professors, and became a beloved icon for the students. After a sports triumph, students headed to the front lawn of Westland to celebrate. Cleveland sometimes came out onto the front porch to say a few words or lead everyone in a cheer. It became a tradition for the students to serenade him on his birthday. At commencements, he walked at the head of the academic procession.

To earn money and keep himself busy, Cleveland wrote articles about his presidency for a wide variety of magazines. He declined to write an autobiography, believing that he was too unpopular for anyone to be interested. In 1900, he accepted a lectureship at Princeton and gave several lectures a year. Later, he became a trustee of the university.

End of the Road

Cleveland maintained a keen interest in the political events of the day. In 1898, he anxiously followed the events leading up to the U.S. declaration of war on Spain, and the brief war that followed. In 1901, he grieved when President McKinley was shot and died of his wounds. His old acquaintance Theodore Roosevelt was sworn in as president.

Gradually, the public's opinion of Cleveland began to change. On March 14, 1900, a currency bill was signed, finally legalizing the gold standard.

The Cleveland family about 1906 with their four surviving children. Their oldest daughter, Ruth, died in 1904.

Theodore Roosevelt, then vice president, wrote that he had come to "realize the very great service you had rendered to the whole country by what you did about free silver. . . . I think you are entitled to thanks and congratulations."

In 1903, Frankie Folsom gave birth to the Clevelands' fifth child, a son named Francis. He joined three older sisters, Ruth, Esther, and Marion, and a four-year-old brother, Richard. Early the next year, however, the oldest daughter, Ruth, died of diphtheria at the age of twelve. Her death was a huge blow to the family. Grover and Frankie decided to sell their summer home in Cape Cod because of the memories of Ruth the house would recall. They bought a house in New Hampshire, where they vacationed with their four remaining children.

Soon Cleveland's health began a steady decline. On the morning of June 24, 1908, he died at his home in Princeton with Frances by his side. Before he died, he said to her, "I have tried so hard to do right."

President Theodore Roosevelt called for 30 days of official mourning. On June 26, a simple, quiet funeral service was held. No eulogy was read, and the service ended with a reading of Cleveland's favorite poem, "Character of the Happy Warrior" by William Wordsworth. Grover Cleveland was buried in Princeton Cemetery next to Ruth's grave. By this time, Cleveland had become a figure held in near-universal respect and admiration.

Grover Cleveland is buried in Princeton, New Jersey, where he and his family lived from his retirement in 1897 to his death in 1908.

Many people today know Cleveland only as the president who served two nonconsecutive terms. But this underappreciated man of courage, honesty, and unyielding conviction deserves a larger place in history. As his biographer Allan Nevins wrote, "It is as a strong man, a man of character, that Cleveland will live in memory." A century after his death, Cleveland's character still shines.

Fast Facts Grover Cleveland

Birth:	March 18, 1837
Birthplace:	Caldwell, New Jersey
Parents:	The Reverend Richard Falley Cleveland and Ann Neal Cleveland
Sisters & Brothers:	Anna (1830–1909) Margaret Louise (1838–1932)
	William Neal (1832–1906) Lewis Frederick (1841–1872)
	Mary Allen (1833–1914) Susan Sophia (1843–?)
	Richard Cecil (1835–1872) Rose Elizabeth (1846–1918)
Education:	Fayetteville Academy, Fayetteville, New York; Clinton Liberal Institute, Clinton, New York
Occupation:	Lawyer
Marriage:	To Frances Folsom, June 2, 1886
Children:	(See First Lady Fast Facts, next page.)
Political Party:	Democratic
Public Offices:	1863–1865 Assistant District Attorney, Erie County, New York
	1871–1873 Sheriff, Erie County, New York
	1882 Mayor, Buffalo, New York
	1883–1884 Governor of New York
	1885–1889 Twenty-second President of the United States
	1893–1897 Twenty-fourth President of the United States
His Vice Presidents:	Thomas A. Hendricks (1885, died November 25, 1885)
	Adlai E. Stevenson (1893–1897)
Major Actions as President:	1886 Dedicated Statue of Liberty
	1887 Signed into law the Interstate Commerce Commission
	1893 Withdrew Hawaiian annexation
	1893 Signed repeal of Sherman Silver Purchase Act
	1894 Called in federal troops to break up Pullman Strike
	1896 Admitted Utah into the nation as the 45th state
Firsts:	First (and only) president born in New Jersey
	First (and only) president to serve two nonconsecutive terms
	First president to marry in the White House
Death:	June 24, 1908
Age at Death:	71 years
Burial Place:	Princeton Cemetery, Princeton, New Jersey

Frances Clara Folsom Cleveland

Birth:	July 21, 1864
Birthplace:	Buffalo, New York
Parents:	Oscar Folsom and Emma Harmon Folsom
Sisters & Brothers:	Nellie (younger sister, died in infancy)
Education:	Wells College (graduated 1885)
Marriage:	To Grover Cleveland, June 2, 1886
Children:	Ruth (1891–1904)
	Esther (1893–1980)
	Marion (1895–1977)
	Richard Folsom (1897–1974)
	Francis Grover (1903–1995)
Firsts:	First to marry a president in the White House
	Youngest first lady
	First to give birth to a child in the White House
Death:	October 29, 1947
Age at Death:	83
Burial Place:	Princeton Cemetery, Princeton, New Jersey

Timeline

1837	1841	1853	1855	1859
Stephen Grover Cleveland born in Caldwell, New Jersey, March 18	Cleveland family moves to Fayetteville, New York	Teaches at the New York Institute for the Blind in New York	Moves to Buffalo, New York; begins to study law	Licensed to practice law

1884	1885	1886	1886	1887
Is Democratic nominee for president; defeats Republican James G. Blaine	Inaugurated 22nd U.S. president, March 4	Marries Frances Folsom at the White House, June 2	Dedicates the Statue of Liberty in New York Harbor	Gives annual message dealing only with the tariff issue

1893	1893	1894	1896	1897
Cleveland calls special session of Congress to repeal the Sherman Silver Purchase Act, June	Has secret operation to remove cancer from mouth, July	Sends federal troops to Chicago to end the Pullman Strike	Utah admitted as the 45th state	Cleveland ends second term, moves to Princeton, New Jersey

1863	1865	1870	1881	1882
Appointed assistant district attorney for Erie County, New York	Defeated in a run for Erie County district attorney	Elected sheriff of Erie County	Elected mayor of Buffalo, New York	Elected governor of New York State

1888	1889	1892	1893	1893
Defeated for reelection by Republican Benjamin Harrison	Becomes an associate in a New York law firm	Reelected president, defeating Benjamin Harrison	Inaugurated 24th U.S. president, March 4	A financial panic begins a long depression, May

1904	1908
Oldest daughter, Ruth, dies of diphtheria	Cleveland dies in Princeton, New Jersey, June 24

Glossary

anarchist: a person who believes that human beings should live without any formal government or who actively tries to destroy existing governments

annex: to add a region or territory to an existing country

bond: a note sold to investors, promising repayment of the purchase price with interest at a later date

depose: to remove from a position of leadership

immigrants: people who come to a country from other countries to live

inauguration: a ceremony in which the president (or other elected executive) officially takes office

labor union: an organization of workers formed to negotiate with management for improved pay or working conditions

legislature: a body of elected representatives that makes laws for a government

lockout: the closing of a plant to union workers by management to resist the the workers' demands

nominate: to name someone to be a candidate for an office

pension: a payment by a government or other employer for past service or sacrifice

ratify: to approve officially

reform: a positive change, especially correction of former abuses of government power

repeal: to legally revoke or annul a law

strike: a work stoppage by workers to force better pay or working conditions

tariff: a tax on goods being brought into a country (import taxes)

veto: in U.S. government, the refusal of the president (or other chief executive) to sign into law a bill passed by Congress (or other legislative body)

Further Reading

★ ★ ★ ★ ★

Collins, David R. *Grover Cleveland: 22nd and 24th President of the United States*. Ada, OK: Garrett Educational Corporation, 1988.

Gaines, Ann Graham. *Grover Cleveland: Our Twenty-Second and Twenty-Fourth President*. Chanhassen, MN: Child's World, 2002.

Sinnott, Susan. *Frances Folsom Cleveland, 1864–1947*. Danbury, CT: Children's Press, 1998.

Williams, Jean Kinney. *Grover Cleveland*. Minneapolis, MN: Compass Point Books, 2003.

MORE ADVANCED READING

Brodsky, Alyn. *Grover Cleveland: A Study in Character*. New York: St. Martin's Press, 2000.

Graff, Henry F. *Grover Cleveland*. New York: Henry Holt, 2002.

Hoyt, Edwin Palmer. *Grover Cleveland*. Chicago: Reilly & Lee, 1962.

Jeffers, H. Paul. *An Honest President: The Life and Presidencies of Grover Cleveland*. New York: Harper Collins, 2000.

Nevins, Allan, *Grover Cleveland: A Study in Courage*. 2 volumes. Newtown, CT: American Political Biography Press, 2002.

Places to Visit

★ ★ ★ ★ ★

**Buffalo and Erie County Historical
Society**
25 Nottingham Court
Buffalo, NY 14216
(716) 873-9644
http://www.bechs.org

Learn about the area where Cleveland began
his political career. The society offers
exhibits and collections of memorabilia,
including such items as Cleveland's
wedding-cake box.

Grover Cleveland Birthplace Museum
207 Bloomfield Avenue
Caldwell, NJ 07006
(973) 226-0001
http://www.westessexguide.com/gcb/

The birthplace of Grover Cleveland is now a
state park and museum. Visitors can see
many of Cleveland's personal belongings,
including his cradle, pipe, wedding hat,
family Bible, and favorite chair.

Princeton University
Princeton, NJ 08544
(609) 258-3000
http://www.princeton.edu

The Cleveland Tower, rising 173 feet (52 m)
above the campus, is named for the former
president.

The White House
1600 Pennsylvania Avenue NW
Washington, DC 20500
Visitors' Office: (202) 456-7041
http://www.whitehouse.gov

Grover Cleveland's home from 1885 to 1889,
and again from 1893 to1897. He and Frances
Folsom were married in the Blue Room on
June 2, 1886.

Online Sites of Interest

★ ★ ★ ★ ★

★ **American Memory, the Library of Congress**

http://memory.loc.gov/ammem/pihtml/pi029.html

This collection of images from presidential inaugurations contains photos of Cleveland's inaugurations and a copy of his 1885 inaugural address in his own handwriting.

★ **The American Presidency**

http://gi.grolier.com/presidents

This site provides biographical information on the presidents at different reading levels, based on material in Scholastic/Grolier encyclopedias.

★ **The American President**

http://www.americanpresident.org

Provides valuable information on the life and times of U.S. presidents. The site is managed by the University of Virginia.

★ **Grover Cleveland Birthplace**

http://www.westessexguide.com/gcb/index.htm

Site offers a biography and historical photos, some rare, of Grover Cleveland.

★ **Internet Public Library, Presidents of the United States (IPL POTUS)**

http://www.ipl.org/div/potus/gcleveland.html

Includes concise information about Cleveland and links to other sites of interest.

★ **Princeton University**

http://etc.princeton.edu/CampusWWW/Companion/cleveland_grover.html

An historical account of Cleveland's days on the Princeton campus.

★ **The White House**

http://www.whitehouse.gov/history/presidents/gc2224.html

Offers a brief biographical article on Grover Cleveland.

Table of Presidents

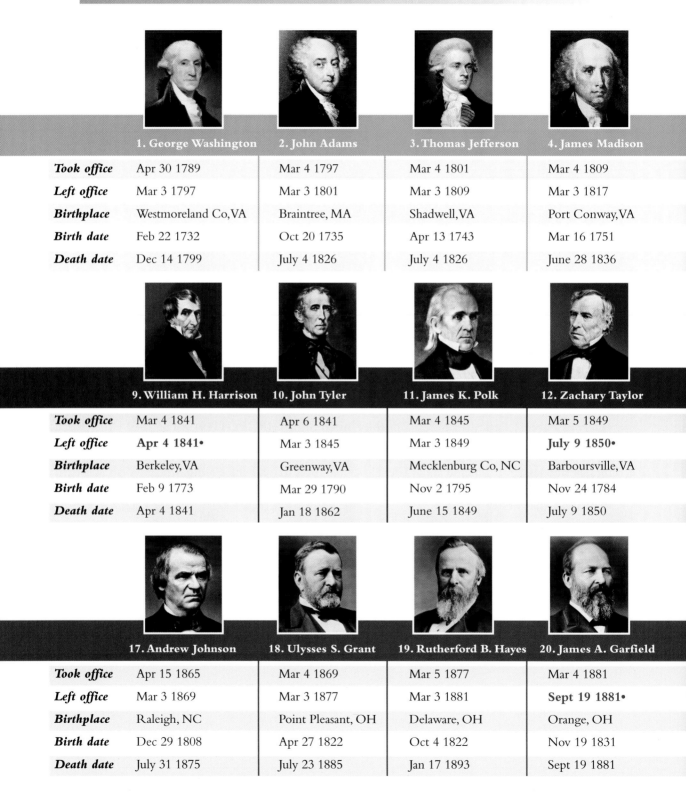

	1. George Washington	2. John Adams	3. Thomas Jefferson	4. James Madison
Took office	Apr 30 1789	Mar 4 1797	Mar 4 1801	Mar 4 1809
Left office	Mar 3 1797	Mar 3 1801	Mar 3 1809	Mar 3 1817
Birthplace	Westmoreland Co, VA	Braintree, MA	Shadwell, VA	Port Conway, VA
Birth date	Feb 22 1732	Oct 20 1735	Apr 13 1743	Mar 16 1751
Death date	Dec 14 1799	July 4 1826	July 4 1826	June 28 1836

	9. William H. Harrison	10. John Tyler	11. James K. Polk	12. Zachary Taylor
Took office	Mar 4 1841	Apr 6 1841	Mar 4 1845	Mar 5 1849
Left office	Apr 4 1841•	Mar 3 1845	Mar 3 1849	July 9 1850•
Birthplace	Berkeley, VA	Greenway, VA	Mecklenburg Co, NC	Barboursville, VA
Birth date	Feb 9 1773	Mar 29 1790	Nov 2 1795	Nov 24 1784
Death date	Apr 4 1841	Jan 18 1862	June 15 1849	July 9 1850

	17. Andrew Johnson	18. Ulysses S. Grant	19. Rutherford B. Hayes	20. James A. Garfield
Took office	Apr 15 1865	Mar 4 1869	Mar 5 1877	Mar 4 1881
Left office	Mar 3 1869	Mar 3 1877	Mar 3 1881	Sept 19 1881•
Birthplace	Raleigh, NC	Point Pleasant, OH	Delaware, OH	Orange, OH
Birth date	Dec 29 1808	Apr 27 1822	Oct 4 1822	Nov 19 1831
Death date	July 31 1875	July 23 1885	Jan 17 1893	Sept 19 1881

5. James Monroe	6. John Quincy Adams	7. Andrew Jackson	8. Martin Van Buren
Mar 4 1817	Mar 4 1825	Mar 4 1829	Mar 4 1837
Mar 3 1825	Mar 3 1829	Mar 3 1837	Mar 3 1841
Westmoreland Co, VA	Braintree, MA	The Waxhaws, SC	Kinderhook, NY
Apr 28 1758	July 11 1767	Mar 15 1767	Dec 5 1782
July 4 1831	Feb 23 1848	June 8 1845	July 24 1862

13. Millard Fillmore	14. Franklin Pierce	15. James Buchanan	16. Abraham Lincoln
July 9 1850	Mar 4 1853	Mar 4 1857	Mar 4 1861
Mar 3 1853	Mar 3 1857	Mar 3 1861	**Apr 15 1865•**
Locke Township, NY	Hillsborough, NH	Cove Gap, PA	Hardin Co, KY
Jan 7 1800	Nov 23 1804	Apr 23 1791	Feb 12 1809
Mar 8 1874	Oct 8 1869	June 1 1868	Apr 15 1865

21. Chester A. Arthur	22. Grover Cleveland	23. Benjamin Harrison	24. Grover Cleveland
Sept 19 1881	Mar 4 1885	Mar 4 1889	Mar 4 1893
Mar 3 1885	Mar 3 1889	Mar 3 1893	Mar 3 1897
Fairfield, VT	Caldwell, NJ	North Bend, OH	Caldwell, NJ
Oct 5 1829	Mar 18 1837	Aug 20 1833	Mar 18 1837
Nov 18 1886	June 24 1908	Mar 13 1901	June 24 1908

	25. William McKinley	**26. Theodore Roosevelt**	**27. William H. Taft**	**28. Woodrow Wilson**
Took office	Mar 4 1897	Sept 14 1901	Mar 4 1909	Mar 4 1913
Left office	**Sept 14 1901•**	Mar 3 1909	Mar 3 1913	Mar 3 1921
Birthplace	Niles, OH	New York, NY	Cincinnati, OH	Staunton, VA
Birth date	Jan 29 1843	Oct 27 1858	Sept 15 1857	Dec 28 1856
Death date	Sept 14 1901	Jan 6 1919	Mar 8 1930	Feb 3 1924

	33. Harry S. Truman	**34. Dwight D. Eisenhower**	**35. John F. Kennedy**	**36. Lyndon B. Johnson**
Took office	Apr 12 1945	Jan 20 1953	Jan 20 1961	Nov 22 1963
Left office	Jan 20 1953	Jan 20 1961	**Nov 22 1963•**	Jan 20 1969
Birthplace	Lamar, MO	Denison, TX	Brookline, MA	Johnson City, TX
Birth date	May 8 1884	Oct 14 1890	May 29 1917	Aug 27 1908
Death date	Dec 26 1972	Mar 28 1969	Nov 22 1963	Jan 22 1973

	41. George Bush	**42. Bill Clinton**	**43. George W. Bush**	
Took office	Jan 20 1989	Jan 20 1993	Jan 20 2001	
Left office	Jan 20 1993	Jan 20 2001	—	
Birthplace	Milton, MA	Hope, AR	New Haven, CT	
Birth date	June 12 1924	Aug 19 1946	July 6 1946	
Death date	—	—	—	

29. Warren G. Harding	30. Calvin Coolidge	31. Herbert Hoover	32. Franklin D. Roosevelt
Mar 4 1921	Aug 2 1923	Mar 4 1929	Mar 4 1933
Aug 2 1923•	Mar 3 1929	Mar 3 1933	**Apr 12 1945•**
Blooming Grove, OH	Plymouth, VT	West Branch, IA	Hyde Park, NY
Nov 21 1865	July 4 1872	Aug 10 1874	Jan 30 1882
Aug 2 1923	Jan 5 1933	Oct 20 1964	Apr 12 1945

37. Richard M. Nixon	38. Gerald R. Ford	39. Jimmy Carter	40. Ronald Reagan
Jan 20 1969	Aug 9 1974	Jan 20 1977	Jan 20 1981
Aug 9 1974★	Jan 20 1977	Jan 20 1981	Jan 20 1989
Yorba Linda, CA	Omaha, NE	Plains, GA	Tampico, IL
Jan 9 1913	July 14 1913	Oct 1 1924	Feb 6 1911
Apr 22 1994	—	—	June 5 2004

• Indicates the president died while in office.

★ Richard Nixon resigned before his term expired.

Index

About the Author

Growing up, Betsy Ochester loved reading and learning about American history and its leaders. That hasn't changed, and Ms. Ochester is pleased to get to bring the story of Grover Cleveland to these pages. She is the author of several history books for young readers, including a previous Encyclopedia of Presidents book, *John Tyler*. Additionally, she has published nine titles in the two Highlights for Children series, *Which Way USA?* and *Top Secret Adventures*, as well as dozens of puzzles, stories, and articles for young readers. Ms. Ochester is a graduate of Cornell University. She lives in Pittsburgh, Pennsylvania, not far from the site of the Homestead Strike of 1892.